Pictures of the Korean War . . .
From the Lens of Cpl. Harold W. Hamilton

First Edition

Written, edited, and compiled by Michael A. Hamilton
Photography by Cpl. Harold W. Hamilton
Pictures printed by permission of Catherine Hamilton

YBDS, LLC

Pictures of the Korean War . . .
From the Lens of Cpl. Harold W. Hamilton

by Michael A. Hamilton

Published by YBDS, LLC, 2415 Old State Road 37 South, Martinsville, IN 46151

ISBN 978-0-9834174-9-1

This book is dedicated to my father, Cpl. Harold W. Hamilton, and all past and present members of the United States Armed Forces.

Table of Contents

Introduction

Sergeant Harold W. Hamilton entered the U.S. Army as a reservist in the 28th Battalion, Company E, 109th, in October of 1950. Initially, he received training in Fort Sheridan, Illinois before being sent to the 28th Battalion. This battalion, which he trained with at Camp Atterbury, IN, consisted mostly of Pennsylvania National Guard. It was inducted into federal service on September 5th, 1950; this was the third activation of these forces in the history of the 28th Battalion. Harold completed training in January of 1951, and as a result, he was one of about 2000 troops re-assigned to units in Korea. The remainder of the 28th Battalion was sent to duty in Germany as a peacekeeping force because, at the time, President Truman was concerned about potential Russian action in Germany, though the United States and Russia had agreed upon division and occupation of Germany after World War II.

Cpl. Hamilton left for Yokohama, Japan from Seattle, WA on March 22nd, 1951, aboard the U.S.N.S. Pvt. Joe P. Martinez. The trip to Yokohama, Japan took 17 days. He was then taken by boat from

Yokohama, Japan to Pusan, South Korea; that trip was 54 hours and landed him in Pusan, South Korea on April 11th, 1951. In Korea, he was reassigned to the 101st Signal Battalion, Company C (Charlie, as he often called it). He indicated the presence of another 101st Signal Battalion which was Company B, (Bravo), but he was in Company C. The 101st Signal Battalion was activated to duty in Korea during August of 1950, although it was considered to be a cadre unit, or a skeleton unit to be built around. He was likely reassigned to this unit due to the tremendous need for signalmen in Korea at that time. He described how they managed to extend signal range by bouncing radio waves off of hill sides, mountainsides, or any other naturally occurring topography that could benefit the signal. He mentioned that the US forces had managed to get a signal from the Korean Peninsula to Japan, which given the technology at that time, was very difficult. With today's technology, that seems like no big deal, but it was immensely advantageous for the U.S./U.N. forces.

Cpl. Hamilton would serve active duty in the Korean War zone until his return home in April of 1952. Harold was a lineman, and was involved with running radio wire and assisting with installing VHF signal wire and repeater stations to relay VHF signals. Signalmen and linemen served as infantry much more in Korea than in all of World War II. This was a result of the fluid nature of the battlefield, with territory being given up frequently by each side. Additionally, signalmen would often have to fight against guerrilla attacks on repeater stations, signal installations and radio wire that would be hidden as much as possible to avoid enemy detection.

Harold arrived in Korea in time to be involved in the spring Chinese offensives, which were ultimately repulsed and the U.S./U.N. forces counter-attacked, pushing the Chinese and North Korean forces back to the eventual stalemate just north of the 38th Parallel. He remained fighting on the front lines until June of 1951, when he and many others were assigned to the reserve for five days of rest and refitting; during rest and refitting, he was in Japan. Among the many places his duty took him in Korea include Seoul, Pocheon, Dongducheon, Chuncheon, and Uijeongbu. The largest city he visited once the IX corps reached the 38th Parallel, in May of 1951, was Chorwon.

Leadership changes occurred rapidly once Harold arrived in Korea in March of 1951. Lt. General Walton H. Walker, the commander of the Eighth Army, was killed in a Jeep accident on December 3rd, 1950. This led to the promotion of General Matthew Ridgway to commander of the Eight Army. When President Truman relieved General Douglas MacArthur from his command on April 11th, 1951, Ridgway was promoted to full general and supreme commander of all U.N. forces in Korea. On April 14th, 1951, General James Van Fleet replaced Ridgway as commander of the U.S. Eight Army and United Nations forces in Korea. Pictures of U.S. Army officers reviewing U.S. and U.N. forces in Korea are pictured later in this book.

Harold's year of active duty in Korea was one of thousands of selfless sacrifices made by United States soldiers. He returned to the United States in March of 1952, with the Korean War at a stalemate since June of 1951. Harold served his remaining active time at Camp Atterbury until July 3rd, 1952. He remained a reservist until he received his discharge from the U.S. Army on October 30th, 1956. After Harold's exit from the Korean theatre of operations, the war remained mostly static until the armistice was signed to cease hostilities on July 27th, 1953. His service in the war zone came during the time where the final outcome was decided. The final dividing parallel changed very little after he left.

During Harold's tenure in Korea, he managed to take over 100 photos depicting subjects from comedian Jack Benny, U.S. Army officers, troop movements, troop reviews, South Korean (ROK) troops, battle action and everyday troop life. The diversity he exhibited in his photographed subjects was representative of the diversity he maintained throughout his life. This book serves to honor his service and all other U.S. servicemen from this bitter, difficult war; additionally, it ensures that the service of Harold and all U.S. troops in Korean are not forgotten in the dust bins of history. The advancement of technology ensures these unpublished photos may now be shared with the world. Readers are encouraged to share anecdotes and comments regarding the 101st Signal Battalion or the Korean War in general on our Facebook page at:

https://www.facebook.com/Pictures-of-the-Korean-War-from-the-Lens-of-Cpl-Harold-Hamilton-246977202829809/?modal=admin_todo_tour

Photo Album

CERTIFICATE OF ACCEPTABILITY

LAST NAME - FIRST NAME - MIDDLE NAME	PRESENT HOME ADDRESS
Hamilton, Harald Wesley	R. R. #3, Martinsville, Ind. Morgan Co.

SELECTIVE SERVICE NUMBER				LOCAL BOARD ADDRESS
12	57	28	10	Indiaa Local Board No. 57 Selecive Service System Armory, 259 E. Morgan St. Martinsville, Indiana

I CERTIFY THAT THE QUALIFICATIONS OF THE ABOVE NAMED REGISTRANT HAVE BEEN CONSIDERED IN ACCORDANCE WITH THE CURRENT REGULATIONS GOVERNING ACCEPTANCE OF SELECTIVE SERVICE REGISTRANTS AND HE WAS THIS DATE:

- [X] FOUND ACCEPTABLE FOR INDUCTION INTO THE ARMED SERVICES
- [ ] FOUND NOT ACCEPTABLE FOR INDUCTION AT THE PRESENT TIME 1/
- [ ] STATUS UNDETERMINED BECAUSE OF INCOMPLETE RECORDS

1/ *Any inquiry relative to personal status should be referred to your Local Board*

(DO NOT USE THIS SPACE)

DATE	PLACE	TYPED OR STAMPED NAME AND GRADE OF JOINT EXAMINING AND INDUCTION STATION COMMANDER	SIGNATURE
20 Aug 50	Indp'ls. Rctg. MS Indianapolis, Ind.	ROBERT M. GUIDICE 1st Lt.USAF	Robert M. Guidice

NME FORM NO 62 1 SEP 48

This is the document that started the journey to Korea for Cpl. Harold W. Hamilton.

28th Battalion photo taken upon completion of training at Camp Atterbury, IN in January 1951

Donald Berkemeier (Pvt-2)
Frank G Salitzky
William R Tyrrell
Richard H. Houston
Wilbur G. Elenbaas Mt. Baines, Michigan
B. J. Tilley
Elmo Branam
Charles Furey
William E Oakley
Woody [illegible]
Pat Walsh Carbondale, Pa.
Gus Wormuth "
Walter Lynady
Joseph Zasik Forest city, Pa.
Tom Davis Haymart Pa
George Seaver West Swanzey, N.H. (Rct)
Don Ward Nashville Ind
Jack Blair Bloomington Ind
Bob Stalz Gary, Indiana
Clifford Beaty Bloomington, Ind.
Kenney Fisher Bloomington, Ind.
Ellis E. Brown Indianapolis, Indiana
[illegible] (Cotton) Purdue Indianapolis Ind [illegible]
Jack Richards Carbondale, Pa.
Herbert C Geb Cadillac Mich.
Morris J. Hardisty Bloomington Ind.
Bill Luther Carbondale, Penna
Jack Davis Cloverdale, Ind.
Ronald Ruane Rome, N.Y.

Harold, second row from top 1st one on left hand side.

Roster of soldiers from previous page includes:
Donald Berkemeier

Frank G. Salitsky
William R. Tyrrell
Richard H. Houston
Wilbur G. Elenbaas, McBain, MI
B.J. Gilley
Elmo Branam
Charles Furey
William Oakley
Pat Walsh, Carbondale, PA
Gus Wormuth
Walter Lynady
Joseph Zosik, Forest City, PA
Tom Davis, Waymart, PA
George Seaver, West Swanzey, PA
Don David, Nashville, TN
Jack Blair, Bloomington, IN
Bob Staltz, Gary, IN
Clifford Beaty, Bloomington, IN
Kenny Fisher, Bloomington, IN
Ellis E. Brown, Indianapolis, IN
"Cotton" Perdue, Indianapolis, IN
Jack Richards, Carbondale, PA
Herbert Jele, Cadillac, MI
Morris Hardisty, Bloomington, IN
Bill Trotter, Carbondale, PA
Jack Davis, Cloverdale, IN
Ronald Ruane, Rome, NY

Soldiers walking by barracks in Camp Atterbury, IN, 1951

Pvt. Leslie Knight of Morgantown, IN poses in front of barracks at Camp Atterbury, IN, 1951

Leslie Knight, Morgantown IN
Jack Miller, Bloomington, IN
Cpl. Harold W. Hamilton, Martinsville, IN
pose in front of train that will take them to Seattle, WA. from Camp Atterbury, IN

Norman Handy, Greencastle, IN
Jack Miller, Bloomington, IN
Cpl. Harold W. Hamilton, Martinsville, IN
pose in front of train that will take them to Seattle, WA. from Camp Atterbury, IN

Norman Handy, Greencastle, IN
Jack Miller, Bloomington, IN
Leslie Knight, Morgantown IN
pose in front of train that will take them to Seattle, WA. from Camp Atterbury, IN

This is a postcard of the U.S.N.S. Pvt. Joe P. Martinez, which is the ship that took Cpl. Hamilton and his fellow troops to Japan, leaving Seattle, WA on March 22nd, 1951. The trip from Seattle, WA to Yokohama, Japan was 17 hours, and was one of the last voyages of the U.S.N.S. Pvt. Joe P. Martinez.

Spent 17 days of on the
Joe P. Martinez. From Seattle to
Yokohama boy we had a time.
Knight wants to tell you something

Pvt Knight
Hello Buddy just a word to
let you know what kind of
a brother you've got he swiped
all the grub they had on the
Martinez and the rest of the guys
went hungry of course I helped
him quite a trip I'll let Harold
finish.

(send home and get my camera)
Leslie Knight from
Morgantown, Indiana

We had three Pints of
Whiskey that night at Music
Hall. I'm with Knight on his
bunk now aboard ship for
Pusan, Korea. These places have
got beer, coke, and whiskey in them

Harold

54 hr. trip by boat from
Yokohama to Pusan
Japan Korea

April 8, 1951

This postcard was sent home to Albert Hamilton, Jr. by Cpl. Harold Hamilton. The troops were en route to Pusan, Korea from Yokohama, Japan on April 8th, 1951. With this dated correspondence, we know Cpl. Hamilton arrived in Pusan on April 11th, 1951. General Douglas MacArthur was removed from his duties as commander of Korean forces the same day.

U.S. Army troops march under watchful eye of their commander, preparing for troop review in Pusan, Korea, April 1951

Troops march under orders of the commander
in Pusan, Korea, April 1951

Troop review in Pusan, Korea, April 1951

U.S./U.N. troops stand at attention for review

U.S./U.N. troops stand at attention for review

Troop review in Pusan, Korea, April 1951

Troop review in Pusan, Korea, April 1951

Marching band in troop review in Pusan, Korea, April 1951

Troop review in Pusan, Korea, April 1951

This picture appears to show General James Van Fleet, the commander of US/UN forces in Korea, reviewing the troops.

Officers stand at attention during review

General James Van Fleet walks to reviewing stand

Cpl. Harold Hamilton in Korea

Cpl. Harold Hamilton and other troops in Jeep

Cpl. Harold Hamilton and unidentified soldier prepare wire in field

Cpl. Harold Hamilton with truck used to haul supplies needed for repeater stations

Harold and others enjoy a respite from the hostilities

Harold and another soldier pose by Jeep

Harold Hamilton poses by Jeep

Harold and fellow soldier in Jeep

Chow time in the field

Harold and other soldiers resting in Jeep

Harold, an unidentified U.S. Army soldier and ROK soldier enjoy chow in field

Chow time for Harold and his fellow troops

Harold heading out to run wire

Harold with his M1 carbine semi-automatic rifle

Harold and another soldier prepare to run wire

Harold again posing with M1 carbine rifle

Radiomen testing connections in the field

Radiomen again testing connections in the field

Soldiers pose in back of Jeep in camp

Cpl. Harold Hamilton poses with a Korean boy in Korean village, summer 1951

A member of the Donkey Squad, important members of the UN Partisan Infantry Forces

A member of the Donkey Squad, important members of the UN Partisan Infantry Forces

Signalman poses on pole

Terminal station at camp – each connected wire allowed connectivity from base to outlying nodes

Empty Jeep in field

Radioman tests signal

Soldiers run signal wire along mountainside

Soldiers test the signal along the rugged mountainside

U.S. flag flies high above base

View from the transport plane as Harold Hamilton is brought into Korean front lines

View of topography in Korea during war

Signalmen rest by Jeep which is hauling signal poles

Aerial views from transport as troops move to base

Aerial view of U.S. Army camp

U.S. Army ordinance explodes on the hillside

U.S. Army convoy of trucks and equipment on the move

Army helicopter and trucks rest idly in camp

Army tanks rest awaiting action

Soldiers examine wire stock

U.S. Army signalmen move out with pole and supplies to establish node of communication to base

U.S. Army soldier poses

Soldiers improvising on barracks

South Korean civilians gather and carry supplies along the main road

Troops crossing river over Army pontoon bridge

Signalmen set up base camp to install another repeater station

Smoke rises from U.S. artillery shelling

Troops and equipment crossing river over Army pontoon bridge

Home sweet home – linesman tents line the hill

This marine, identified as "our boy Don", of the Marine 1st Battalion, 7th Infantry, 3rd Division poses at the "No Name Line" in Korea north of Seoul

South Korean ROK troops pose for Sgt. Hamilton

More South Korean ROK troops want in the picture, so Cpl. Hamilton obliges his allies

Coffee, chow and a cigarette in camp

Soldiers near a river had a luxury: an opportunity to bathe and wash clothes, as this soldier is doing.

U.S. and South Korean ROK troops pose

U.S. soldier with bazooka takes aim at the target

U.S. soldier with bazooka takes aim at the target

Soldiers head to river to bathe and wash clothes

U.S. tanks prepare to be ferried across the river

U.S. howitzers prepare to fire

U.S. howitzers prepare to fire

Destroyed U.S. Army Jeep from battle

Destroyed U.S. Army Jeep from battle

Dug in U.S. Army howitzer ready for combat

U.S. Army tank and troops on the move

U.S. Army 155mm self-propelled howitzer

Troops salute U.S. officers passing in Jeep

Soldiers pose with their Jeep – and road kill

Troops enjoy a break before resuming trench work

Army troops enjoy a card game

Moving into another Korean village below

Harold and another soldier plot strategy

This picture represents the unknown that the U.S. Army signalmen faced in daily duties

U.S. Army Jeep on narrow road along cliff

Haircut time at camp for this soldier

Jack Benny entertains U.S. troops in Korea during the Korean War in summer of 1951. Armistice talks had begun at this point . . .

Soldiers enjoy boxing for recreation . . .

. . . before realizing it is more fun watching the two South Korean boys go at it

U.S. troops support the South Korean boys spirit while soldier referees

Men and equipment prepared to move out on next mission

Soldiers clown for picture

Troops rest while discussing next move

A picture of the frigid winter of 1951 in Korea

Units at work as helicopter prepares to land during the Korean winter of 1951-52

Troops paddle across river during Korean
Winter of 1951-52

U.S. Army helicopter sits idly

Units at work after helicopter lands
during the Korean winter of 1951-52

Units at work after helicopter lands during the Korean winter of 1951-52

Units at work as helicopter prepares to land

Soldier smokes outside winter barracks during the winter of 1951-52 in Korea.

Soldiers guard the road into and out of base camp

141413
日本銀行券
壹圓
日本銀行
141413
日本銀行券
壹圓
日本銀行
1 YEN
1 YEN

South Korean money from wartime, signed by:
Pfc. Raymond Adelsbarger
Pfc. James Davis
Pfc. Bill O'Keefe
Pfc. Kenneth Larman
Cpl. Sam Young
Sgt. N. Cartsmel, Barbeston, OH
Sgt. James Couch

Honorable Discharge

from the Armed Forces of the United States of America

This is to certify that

Cpl, Harold W. Hamilton, ER 55 031 716, Inf USAR, Ready Reserve, (Active Status), Who was inducted 4 Oct 50 and transferred to USAR 4 Jul 52

was Honorably Discharged from the

Army of the United States

on the 30th day of October 1956 This certificate is awarded as a testimonial of Honest and Faithful Service

ROBERT I. REMSNYDER
Major, Adjutant General's Corps

The end of the journey . . . Cpl. Harold W. Hamilton received his honorable discharge from the U.S. Army on October 30th, 1956.

Cpl. Harold W. Hamilton

January 15th, 1928 – March 12th, 1997

www.ingramcontent.com/pod-product-compliance
Lightning Source LLC
Chambersburg PA
CBHW081427090426
42740CB00017B/3210
* 9 7 8 0 9 8 3 4 1 7 4 9 1 *